Presented to

By

On the Occasion of

Date

© 2009 by Barbour Publishing, Inc.

Compiled by Marla Tipton.

ISBN 978-1-60260-615-9

Text was compiled from the following: *365 Meditations for the Satisfied Soul, 365 Days to Greater Faith, 365 Days on My Knees, 365 Days of Faith, 365 Days of Joy, 365 Days of Praise, 365 Everyday Prayers, 365 Inspirational Quotes, Spiritual Refreshment for Women: Everyday Blessings, Spiritual Refreshment for Women: Everyday Encouragement,* and *Spiritual Refreshment for Women: Everyday Prayers,* published by Barbour Publishing, Inc.

Published by Barbour Publishing, Inc., P.O. Box 719, Uhrichsville, Ohio 44683, www.barbourbooks.com.

Our mission is to publish and distribute inspirational products offering exceptional value and biblical encouragement to the masses.

Member of the
Evangelical Christian
Publishers Association

Printed in India.

WHISPERS OF
Faith

BARBOUR
PUBLISHING

Guide Me

Send forth your light and your truth, let them guide me; let them bring me to your holy mountain, to the place where you dwell. Then will I go to the altar of God, to God, my joy and my delight. I will praise you with the harp, O God, my God.

PSALM 43:3–4 NIV

Forgiveness

Make a clean break with all
cutting, backbiting, profane
talk. Be gentle with one another,
sensitive. Forgive one another as
quickly and thoroughly as God in
Christ forgave you.

EPHESIANS 4:31–32 MSG

Faith, like Light

A tried saint brings more glory
to God than an untried one.
Faith, like light, should always be
simple and unbending; while love,
like warmth, should beam forth
on every side and bend to every
necessity of our brethren.

MARTIN LUTHER

Never Alone

What God has called you to
accomplish in your life, He has not
called you to accomplish alone. He
is always there, providing you with
the resources you need to get the
job done. . . . Whether you need
wisdom, inspiration, confidence,
strength, or just plain tenacity, you
will find your answer in Him.

Childlike Faith

It is a masterpiece of the devil
to make us believe that children
cannot understand religion.
Would Christ have made a child
the standard of faith if He had
known that it was not capable of
understanding His words?

D. L. MOODY

You Matter!

[God] wants you to be assured that
He will always be there for you.
You need not fear that He will
grow tired of you, lose interest,
and abandon you. You are precious
to Him, no matter your age, your
condition, your circumstances.
You matter to Him.

Plans for Your Life

May God's love guide you through the special plans He has for your life.

I look behind me and you're there, then up ahead and you're there, too—your reassuring presence, coming and going. This is too much, too wonderful—I can't take it all in!

PSALM 139:5–6 MSG

God's Promises

We may. . .depend upon God's
promises, for. . .He will be as good
as His word. He is so kind that He
cannot deceive us, so true that He
cannot break His promise.

MATTHEW HENRY

Help Me to Remember

In times of violent emotions,
Lord, help me to remember Your
unending forgiveness and to treat
others with the kindness and
compassion You show me every
day of my life. Amen.

Victory—Our Faith

I should never have known the Savior's love half as much if I had not been in the storms of affliction. "Whatever is born of God overcomes the world; and this is the victory that has overcome the world—our faith" (1 John 5:4 NASB).

At Calvary

Not only do You give me all I need,
but You also provided this earth for
us to live on. Nothing really belongs
to me, yet how You shower Your
blessings upon me to enjoy.

O the love that drew
salvation's plan!
O the grace that brought
it down to man!
O the mighty gulf that
God did span
At Calvary.

WILLIAM REED NEWELL

WHISPERS OF
Faith

Reconciled

Once you were alienated from
God. . . . But now he has
reconciled you by Christ's physical
body through death to present you
holy in his sight, without blemish
and free from accusation—if you
continue in your faith, established
and firm, not moved from the
hope held out in the gospel.

COLOSSIANS 1:21–23 NIV

Ask in Faith

Ask in faith, nothing wavering.
For he that wavereth is like a wave
of the sea driven with the wind
and tossed.

JAMES 1:6 KJV

A Wonderful Father

For [God] is, indeed, a wonderful
Father who longs to pour out His
mercy upon us, and whose majesty
is so great that He can transform
us from deep within.

TERESA OF AVILA

Help!

When you need help, bring every concern before your Lord. Then trust God and thank Him that He will come through for you—in His time.

Give us help from trouble: for vain is the help of man.

PSALM 60:11 KJV

His Mighty Acts

Great is the LORD, and highly to
be praised, and His greatness is
unsearchable. One generation
shall praise Your works to another,
and shall declare Your mighty acts.

PSALM 145:3–4 NASB

Faith in God

There are no dilemmas out of
which you shall not be delivered if
you live near to God. He goes not
amiss who goes in the company of
God. Every man lives by faith, the
nonbeliever as well as the saint;
the one by faith in natural laws
and the other by faith in God.

A. W. TOZER

My Shepherd

You control the beginning and end
of all that lives. You have given
me the present, and You lay out
my future before me. Thank You,
Lord, for being my Shepherd.
Thank You for watching over and
protecting me as a shepherd does
his sheep.

Acceptance

A man can accept what Christ has done without knowing how it works; indeed, he certainly won't know how it works until he's accepted it.

C. S. LEWIS

Joys of Life

Friendship is one of the sweetest
joys of life. Many might have failed
beneath the bitterness of their trial
had they not found a friend.

CHARLES H. SPURGEON

His Great Power

Ah, Sovereign LORD, you have
made the heavens and the earth by
your great power and outstretched
arm. Nothing is too hard for you.

JEREMIAH 32:17 NIV

His Reflection

Heavenly Father, the next time
I am prepared to lash out at
someone who has hurt me, let Your
forgiveness and love be reflected
in my response. "A soft answer
turneth away wrath: but grievous
words stir up anger"(Proverbs
15:1 KJV).

A Gift

For by grace you have been saved
through faith, and this is not your
own doing; it is the gift of God.

EPHESIANS 2:8 NRSV

You Care

Father, I marvel that You know
me so well. You count the hairs on
my head. You care about the pain I
experience. When a sparrow falls,
You care. How much, then, You
must care for me.

Overcoming

The Bible says we will encounter trials in this life. After all, this world is not our home; it's just a temporary residence. While we are here, though, God promised His presence, love, and comfort. He will walk beside you and give you strength to overcome whatever is in your path.

Morning Star

From far beyond our world of
trouble and care and change, our
Lord shines with undimmed light,
a radiant, guiding Star to all who
will follow Him—a morning Star,
promise of a better day.

CHARLES E. HURLBURT AND T. C. HORTON

Excellent and Eternal Being

The celestial order and beauty of
the universe compel me to admit
that there is some excellent and
eternal Being who deserves the
respect and homage of men.

CICERO

Your Faith Will Grow

God has called you to live a life
of vibrant faith, open to His
direction, keeping your eyes on
Him. Day by day you will see His
faithfulness, and your faith will
grow.

Sustaining Faith

Faith is to the soul what life is
to the body. Prayer is to faith
what breath is to the body. How a
person can live and not breathe is
past my comprehension, and how a
person can believe and not pray is
past my comprehension, too.

J. C. RYLE

Youthfulness

Let no one look down on your
youthfulness, but rather in speech,
conduct, love, faith and purity,
show yourself an example of those
who believe.

1 TIMOTHY 4:12 NASB

Seek and Desire You

Lord Jesus Christ, let me seek You
by desiring You, and let me desire
You by seeking You; let me find
You by loving You and love You in
finding You.

ANSELM

Joy of the Lord

[God] knows everything about us.
And He cares about everything.
Moreover, He can manage every
situation. And He loves us!
Surely this is enough to open the
wellsprings of joy. . . . And joy is
always a source of strength.

HANNAH WHITALL SMITH

Test of Our Faith

The test of our faith in the
promises of God is never found in
the easygoing, comfortable ways of
life, but in the great emergencies,
the times of storm and of stress,
the days of adversity, when all
human aid fails.

ETHEL BELL

Our Creator

Do you not know? Have you not heard? The LORD is the everlasting God, the Creator of the ends of the earth. He will not grow tired or weary, and his understanding no one can fathom. He gives strength to the weary and increases the power of the weak.

ISAIAH 40:28–29 NIV

Founded like a Church

The historic glory of America lies
in the fact that it is the one nation
that was founded like a church.
That is, it was founded on a faith
that was not merely summed up
after it had existed but was defined
before it existed.

G. K. CHESTERTON

Faith = Power of God

My speech and my proclamation
were not with plausible words of
wisdom, but with a demonstration
of the Spirit and of power, so
that your faith might rest not on
human wisdom but on the power
of God.

1 CORINTHIANS 2:4–5 NRSV

Blessing

Bless the LORD, O my soul: and
all that is within me, bless his holy
name. Bless the LORD, O my soul,
and forget not all his benefits:
who forgiveth all thine iniquities;
who healeth all thy diseases;
who redeemeth thy life from
destruction; who crowneth thee
with lovingkindness and tender
mercies.

PSALM 103:1–4 KJV

Evidence

Faith does not mean believing
without evidence. It means
believing in realities that go
beyond sense and sight—for which
a totally different sort of evidence
is required.

JOHN BAILLIE

Never-Failing Love

Lord God, my faith in You is not
based in my senses or my intellect
but in Your never-failing love,
which saved my soul and promises
me unspeakable joy. Amen.

An Instrument

Lord, make me an instrument of
   Your peace.
Where there is hatred,
   let me bring love.
Where there is offense,
   forgiveness.
Where there is discord,
   reconciliation.
Where there is doubt, faith.
Where there is despair, hope.
Where there is sadness, joy.
Where there is darkness,
   Your light.

FRANCIS OF ASSISI

Be Alive

Life is what we are alive to. It is
not length but breadth. . . .
Be alive to. . .goodness, kindness,
purity, love, history, poetry, music,
flowers, stars, God, and eternal
hope.

MALTBIE D. BABCOCK

Thy Redeeming Love

Come, Thou Fount of every blessing,
tune my heart to sing Thy grace;
Streams of mercy, never ceasing,
call for songs of loudest praise.
Teach me some melodious sonnet,
sung by flaming tongues above;
Praise the mount—I'm fixed upon
it—mount of Thy redeeming love.

ROBERT ROBINSON

Faith before Feeling

Sight is not faith, and hearing is
not faith, neither is feeling faith;
but believing when we neither
see, hear, nor feel is faith; and
everywhere the Bible tells us
our salvation is to be by faith.
Therefore we must believe before
we feel, and often against our
feelings, if we would honor God by
our faith.

HANNAH WHITALL SMITH

Fruit

But the fruit of the Spirit is love,
joy, peace, patience, kindness,
goodness, faithfulness, gentleness
and self-control. Against such
things there is no law.

GALATIANS 5:22–23 NIV

Your Heart

God makes our lives a medley of
joy and tears, hope and help, love
and encouragement. Where your
pleasure is, there is your treasure:
where your treasure, there your
heart; where your heart, there your
happiness.

AUGUSTINE

Trust in You

Though I may not know the
outcome of everything in my life,
dear Father, I am trusting in You,
and I know You care for all my
needs. How my heart rejoices that
I can trust in You! Amen.

Deliverance

God has delivered you; give Him
your gratitude. He is delivering
you; give Him your confidence. He
will deliver you; give Him your joy.
Faith is a strong power, mastering
any difficulty in the strength of
the Lord who made heaven and
earth.

CORRIE TEN BOOM

Fill Us

Open wide the windows of our
spirits and fill us full of light; open
wide the door of our hearts, that we
may receive and entertain Thee with
all our powers of adoration.

CHRISTINA ROSSETTI

Even Today

Today Jesus is working just as
wonderful works as when He
created the heavens and the
earth. His wondrous grace, His
wonderful omnipotence, is for His
child who needs Him and who
trusts Him, even today.

CHARLES E. HURLBURT AND T. C. HORTON

Lamb of God

The Christian faith engages the
profoundest problems the human
mind can entertain and solves
them completely and simply by
pointing to the Lamb of God.

A. W. TOZER

Know God

Those men who know God the
best are those who meditate most
upon Him. The man who possesses
"the joy of the Lord" finds it
his strength, in that it fortifies
him against temptation. Faith is
believing where we cannot prove.

ALFRED, LORD TENNYSON

A Cheerful Giver

Guide me as I choose among many
worthy causes; make me conscious
of the blessings You have given
me, Lord. Help me to be a cheerful
giver. Amen.

True Happiness

The warmth of a friend's presence
brings joy to our hearts, sunlight
to our souls, and pleasure to all of
life. Happiness is inward and not
outward; and so it does not depend
on what we have, but on what we are.

HENRY VAN DYKE

God Alone

We readily acknowledge that God
alone is to be the rule and measure
of our prayers. In our prayers we
are to look totally unto Him and
act totally for Him, and we must
pray in this manner and for such
ends as are suitable to His glory.

WILLIAM LAW

Our Unlimited Love

Everything which relates to God
is infinite. We must, therefore,
while we keep our hearts humble,
keep our aims high. Our highest
services are indeed but finite,
imperfect. But as God is unlimited
in goodness, He should have our
unlimited love.

HANNAH MORE

A Grand Cathedral

Christian faith is a grand
cathedral, with divinely pictured
windows. Standing without, you
see no glory, nor can imagine
any. But standing within, every
ray of light reveals a harmony of
unspeakable splendors.

NATHANIEL HAWTHORNE

Sing

I will sing unto the LORD as long
as I live: I will sing praise to my
God while I have my being. My
meditation of him shall be sweet:
I will be glad in the LORD.

PSALM 104:33–34 KJV

Through Him

I do desire for my fellow
Christians and for myself that
more and more the great object
of our thoughts, motives, and
acts may be "Jesus only." "In all
these things we overwhelmingly
conquer through Him who loved
us" (Romans 8:37 NASB).

Body of Christ

In many ways the members of my
church family are more different
than we are alike, yet Your love for
us knows no human boundaries.
We are family. We are Your church,
Lord. Unify us with Your love.
Amen.

When We're Pleased

In almost everything that touches our everyday life on earth, God is pleased when we're pleased. He wills that we be as free as birds to soar and sing our Maker's praise without anxiety.

A. W. TOZER

A Presence

And I have felt
A presence that disturbs
   me with the joy
Of elevated thoughts;
   a sense sublime
Of something far more
   deeply interfused,
Whose dwelling is the
   light of setting suns.

WILLIAM WORDSWORTH

Tell Jesus

There is not a thought, a feeling, or a circumstance with which you may not go and tell Jesus. There is nothing that you may not, in the confidence of love and in the simplicity of faith, tell Jesus.

OCTAVIUS WINSLOW

Greatest Proof

The greatest proof of Christianity
for others is not how far a man
can logically analyze his reasons
for believing, but how far in
practice he will stake his life on
his belief.

T. S. ELIOT

Give to the Lord

Give unto the LORD, O ye mighty,
give unto the LORD glory and
strength. Give unto the LORD the
glory due unto his name; worship
the LORD in the beauty of holiness.

PSALM 29:1–2 KJV

United with Christ

Regret looks back. Faith unites
the soul with Christ as a bride
is united with her bridegroom.
Everything that they have is held
in common, whether good or evil.
So the believer can boast of and
glory in whatever Christ possesses
as though it were his or her own.

MARTIN LUTHER

Pursue, Fight, Take Hold

Pursue righteousness, godliness, faith, love, endurance, gentleness. Fight the good fight of the faith; take hold of the eternal life, to which you were called.

1 TIMOTHY 6:11–12 NRSV

I Will Follow

Lord, the task is impossible for
me but not for Thee. Lead the way
and I will follow. Why should I
fear? I am on a royal mission. I am
in the service of the King of kings.

MARY SLESSOR

Nothing Can Separate

For I am persuaded, that neither
death, nor life, nor angels, nor
principalities, nor powers, nor
things present, nor things to come,
nor height, nor depth, nor any
other creature, shall be able to
separate us from the love of God,
which is in Christ Jesus our Lord.

ROMANS 8:38–39 KJV

No Other

The Lord our God is with us, as
He was with our fathers; may He
not leave us or forsake us, so that
He may incline our hearts to Him,
to walk in all His ways. . .that all
the peoples of the earth may know
that the Lord is God; there is no
other.

GEORGE HERBERT WALKER BUSH

Never a Needless Tear

When we believe that God is Father, we also believe that such a Father's hand will never cause His child a needless tear. We may not understand life any better, but we will not resent life any longer.

WILLIAM BARCLAY

Unchangeable

If the Lord be with us, we have no
cause of fear. His eye is upon us,
His arm over us, His ear open to
our prayer—His grace sufficient,
His promise unchangeable.

JOHN NEWTON

His Grace

We are not meant to be seen as God's perfect, bright-shining examples, but to be seen as the everyday essence of ordinary lives exhibiting the miracle of His grace.

OSWALD CHAMBERS

Fruitfulness

No matter what your
circumstances are, God has a plan
for you, and that plan is not out of
reach. As long as you are looking
to Him, your life will be fruitful
and fulfilling. That's His will, His
promise, His plan.

A Content Heart

The heart is rich when it is
content, and it is always content
when its desires are fixed on
God. Nothing can bring greater
happiness than doing God's will
for the love of God.

MIGUEL FEBRES CORDERO-MUÑOZ

No Struggle

It is blessed when we can praise God when the sun has gone down, when darkness lowers and trials multiply. Faith does not struggle; faith lets God do it all.

CORRIE TEN BOOM

A Bright Future

The road ahead may not be
easy, but it will be the greatest
adventure, the greatest race you've
ever attempted. And best of all,
the destination is certain. Throw
yourself unreservedly into the
work that God has called you to.
Take hold of your future with both
hands.

A Searchlight

Dark as my path may seem to
others, I carry a magic light in my
heart. Faith, the spiritual strong
searchlight, illumines the way, and
although sinister doubts lurk in
the shadow, I walk unafraid toward
the enchanted wood where the
foliage is always green, where joy
abides. . .in the presence of the
Lord.

HELEN KELLER

Perfect Faithfulness

O LORD, you are my God; I will
exalt you and praise your name,
for in perfect faithfulness you have
done marvelous things, things
planned long ago.

ISAIAH 25:1 NIV

God Is with You

"The LORD your God is with you,
he is mighty to save. He will take
great delight in you, he will quiet
you with his love, he will rejoice
over you with singing."

ZEPHANIAH 3:17 NIV

His Comfort

Mighty Lord in heaven, grief
overwhelms me. I feel alone, even
in the midst of friends and family
who have come to comfort me.
Thank You for the comfort only
You can give. Amen.

Endless Good

We walk without fear, full of hope
and courage and strength to do
His will, waiting for the endless
good which He is always giving as
fast as He can get us able to take
it in.

GEORGE MACDONALD

My All

Jesus, my Shepherd, Guardian,
Friend, my Prophet, Priest, and
King, my Lord, my Life, my Way,
my End, accept the praise I bring.

JOHN NEWTON

Walk in Him

Therefore as you have received
Christ Jesus the Lord, so walk in
Him, having been firmly rooted
and now being built up in Him
and established in your faith,
just as you were instructed, and
overflowing with gratitude.

COLOSSIANS 2:6–7 NASB

More like Thee

More faith in my Savior,
  more sense of His care;
More joy in His service,
  more purpose in prayer. . . .
More fit for the kingdom,
  more used would I be;
More blessed and holy,
  more, Savior, like Thee.

PHILIP P. BLISS

Creation

Our God cares about details. You
see it throughout His creation. . . .
When you wonder if God is interested
in the details of your life, consider the
evidence demonstrated in nature. He
cares about everything—no matter how
inconsequential.

Expect

Reflect on God's goodness.
Be thankful for all He's given.
Be joyful and at peace. Always be
in a state of expectancy, and see
that you leave room for God to
come in as He likes.

OSWALD CHAMBERS

Do Something

A true faith in Jesus Christ will
not suffer us to be idle. No, it is an
active, lively, restless principle;
it fills the heart so that it cannot
be easy till it is doing something
for Jesus Christ.

GEORGE WHITEFIELD

Faith, Not Reason

Reason must be deluded, blinded, and destroyed. Faith must trample underfoot all reason, sense, and understanding, and whatever it sees must be put out of sight and. . . [know] nothing but the Word of God.

MARTIN LUTHER

Faithful Narrative

God is writing a story of faith
through your life. What will it
describe? . . . Whatever your
account says, if you love Jesus, the
end is never in question. Those
who love Him finish in heaven,
despite their trials on earth. . . .
Today, write a chapter in your
faithful narrative of God's love.

PAMELA McQUADE

Draw Near

Let us draw near with a true heart
in full assurance of faith, having
our hearts sprinkled from an evil
conscience, and our bodies washed
with pure water.

HEBREWS 10:22 KJV

Just Wait

God won't withhold from you just
to be cruel or make a point, but
He does see the big picture and
knows the right when, where, and
how. So don't get anxious; just
wait. You will see what God has
promised you—all in due time.

He Opens the Way

Faith looks up and sails on. . .
not seeing one shoreline or
earthly lighthouse. . . . Often
our way seems to lead into utter
uncertainty or even darkness and
disaster. But He opens the way,
making our midnight hours the
very gates of day.

A. B. SIMPSON

The Sun

Even in winter, even in the midst
of the storm, the sun is still there.
Somewhere, up above the clouds,
it still shines and warms and pulls
at the life buried deep inside the
brown branches and frozen earth.
The sun is there! Spring will come!
The clouds cannot stay forever.

GLORIA GAITHER

God Knows

You do not know what you are
going to do; the only thing you
know is that God knows what He
is doing. . . . It is this attitude that
keeps you in perpetual wonder—
you do not know what God is
going to do next.

OSWALD CHAMBERS

Full of Wonder

Every moment is full of wonder,
and God is always present. We
have a Father in heaven who is
almighty, who loves His children
as He loves His only begotten Son,
and whose very joy and delight it
is to. . .help them at all times and
under all circumstances.

GEORGE MUELLER

The Source of
All Good Things

Dear Father, may my words today
show that I recognize You as
the source of all good things. I
appreciate Your mercy toward me.
Amen.

Real Love

Love never gives up. Love cares
more for others than for self.
Love. . .puts up with anything,
trusts God always, always looks
for the best, never looks back, but
keeps going to the end.

1 CORINTHIANS 13:4, 7 MSG

Life

"I have been crucified with Christ; and it is no longer I who live, but Christ lives in me; and the life which I now live in the flesh I live by faith in the Son of God, who loved me and gave Himself up for me."

GALATIANS 2:20 NASB

Never Leave or Forsake

Father, this crazy, out-of-control
world seems to be getting worse all
the time. We are pressed in with
problems, crime, uncertainty, and
fear on every side. You promised
You would never leave or forsake
us. I know You take us by the hand
each day, gently leading us through
the good times and the bad.

Beyond Evidence

Faith does not mean believing
without evidence. It means
believing in realities that go
beyond sense and sight—for which
a totally different sort of evidence
is required.

JOHN BAILLIE

My Vision

Be Thou my Vision,
  O Lord of my heart;
Naught be all else to me,
  save that Thou art.
Thou my best thought,
  by day or by night,
Waking or sleeping,
  Thy presence my light.

CELTIC TRADITIONAL

All You Need

[God] is the provider of all you
need. If you need joy, He'll give it
to you with enough to share. If you
need wisdom, it's there for you as
well. Whatever you have on your
list—ask Him for it. Then trust
Him.

Peace

Instead of focusing on differences
of opinions, Lord, help me look to
You, my perfect Brother. Then the
small things my Christian brothers
and sisters do will not make me
stumble and the large issues will be
settled. Amen.

Never Quit

You've always been great toward
me—what love! . . . You, O God,
are both tender and kind, not
easily angered, immense in love,
and you never, never quit.

PSALM 86:13, 15 MSG

Blessing

Through Christ Jesus, God has
blessed the Gentiles with the same
blessing he promised to Abraham,
so that we who are believers might
receive the promised Holy Spirit
through faith.

GALATIANS 3:14 NLT

Expect and Believe!

God knows your heart. The One who holds the future in His hands sees your faithfulness. He has entrusted you with much responsibility because He knows He can count on you. He will reward you and will bring you into a place of blessing. Expect it and believe He'll do it. God applauds you!

Praise

The thought of You stirs us so deeply that we cannot be content unless we praise You, because You have made us for yourself, and our hearts find no peace until they rest in You.

AUGUSTINE

Facing Trials

My brothers and sisters, whenever
you face trials of any kind,
consider it nothing but joy,
because you know that the testing
of your faith produces endurance;
and let endurance have its full
effect, so that you may be mature
and complete, lacking in nothing.

JAMES 1:2–4 NRSV

My Church

May my church be graced, Lord,
with a special sincerity that shows
the world Your love. May Your
grace shine out to all who meet us.
Amen.

Ordinary People

God has always used ordinary
people to carry out His
extraordinary mission. Anything
that exists in any way must
necessarily have its origin in God.

THOMAS AQUINAS

A Living Faith

If we desire to praise God more, we must ask for grace that our private devotions may rise to a higher standard. A living faith is not something you have to carry but something that carries you.

J. H. OLDHAM

No Denying

Sometimes our faith fails, but Jesus never does. When we change for the worse, slip, or make a mistake, He is still the same faithful God He's always been. Though we may falter, He cannot. . . . If we have trusted Him, we can return to Him for renewed forgiveness. His own faithfulness will not allow Him to deny us.

PAMELA MCQUADE

Let Love Shine

Let Jesus be in your heart, eternity
in your spirit, the world under
your feet, the will of God in your
actions. And let the love of God
shine forth from you.

CATHERINE OF GENOA

All Is Right

The happiness of life is made up
of little things—a smile, a hug, a
moment of shared laughter. The
year's at the spring and day's at the
morn. . .God's in His heaven—
all's right with the world!

ROBERT BROWNING

Faith in Tomorrow

You promise that all bad things
come to an end. Until then,
Father, give me contentment with
the blessings I have and faith in
tomorrow. Amen.

Impossible

It is impossible to please God without faith. Anyone who wants to come to him must believe that God exists and that he rewards those who sincerely seek him.

HEBREWS 11:6 NLT

My Wisdom

Teach me, O Lord, to do Your will; teach me to live worthily and humbly in Your sight; for You are my Wisdom, who know me truly, and who knew me before the world was made, and before I had my being.

THOMAS À KEMPIS

Things of This World

Happy is the one who has learned to hold the things of this world with a loose grip. Of all classes and descriptions of persons on this earth, they are the happiest of whom it may be said that the things most hoped for by them are the things not seen.

MENNONITE WRITINGS

Contentment

I know You want the best for me,
Lord, and You will provide it. My
job is to live my life in a way that
glorifies You. Everything beyond
that is a blessing. I choose to be
content. Amen.

WHISPERS OF
Faith

Direction

I find the great thing in this world
is not so much where we stand, as
in what direction we are moving.
To reach the port of heaven, we
must sail sometimes with the wind
and sometimes against it—but we
must sail, and not drift, nor lie at
anchor.

OLIVER WENDELL HOLMES

Great Reward

Someone does take notice of all
you do. Your heavenly Father is
watching even when it seems no
one notices. He's proud of you and
appreciates all you do. You show
the love and life of God to those
around you. Take heart—God is
your exceedingly great reward.

Hidden Treasures

The human heart has
   hidden treasures,
In secret kept, in silence sealed—
The thoughts, the hopes,
   the dreams, the pleasures,
Whose charms were broken
   if revealed.

CHARLOTTE BRONTË

Let the Lord Choose

Love must cooperate with faith
and cast out fear, so that the soul
may have boldness before God.
The sweetest lesson I have learned
in God's school is to let the Lord
choose for me.

D. L. MOODY

WHISPERS OF
Faith

Done in Secret

"And when you pray, do not be like the hypocrites, for they love to pray standing in the synagogues and on the street corners to be seen by men. . . . But when you pray, go into your room, close the door and pray to your Father, who is unseen. Then your Father, who sees what is done in secret, will reward you."

MATTHEW 6:5–6 NIV

Sure Steps

The more you know [God], the
more quickly you know His
will and His ways and can more
assuredly step out in faith toward
His righteous cause. Your steps are
sure because your path is well lit
with the goodness of God. You're
on the right path.

Soul Satisfaction

Satisfaction is the result of a
job well done. Sometimes your
expectation for the blessings of
God requires you to press a little
harder and stretch your faith a
little farther to see the results
you've asked God for. You can
be sure all your efforts will be
rewarded. God promises to satisfy
your soul—a deep satisfaction
only He can provide.

Love of Wonder

Whether sixty or sixteen, there
is in every human being's heart
the love of wonder, the sweet
amazement at the stars and
starlike things, the undaunted
challenge of events, the unfailing
childlike appetite for what-next,
and the joy of the game of living.

SAMUEL ULLMAN

Fly

When you come to the edge of all the light you know and are about ready to step off into the darkness of the unknown, faith is knowing that one of two things will happen: There will be something solid to stand on, or you will be taught how to fly.

BARBARA J. WINTER

God Is. . .

God is sufficiently wise and good and powerful and merciful to turn even the most apparently disastrous events to the advantage and profit of those who humbly adore and accept His will in all that He permits.

JEAN-PIERRE DE CAUSSADE

Spiritual Certainty

There is more than one way of seeing. We view the world around us with our eyes, but by doing so, we don't apprehend all there is in life. Those things we "see" by faith cannot be envisioned by our physical eyes. . . . But when God speaks to our hearts, it is as real as if we'd viewed the truth plainly in front of us. Like Paul, though our eyes cannot see it, we have spiritual certainty.

PAMELA MCQUADE

Grace of God

*The grace of God means
something like:*

Here is your life. You might never
have been, but you are, because the
party wouldn't have been complete
without you. Here is the world.
Beautiful and terrible things will
happen. Don't be afraid. I am with
you.

FREDERICK BUECHNER

Rest Assured

Know therefore that the LORD thy
God, he is God, the faithful God,
which keepeth covenant and mercy
with them that love him and keep
his commandments to a thousand
generations.

DEUTERONOMY 7:9 KJV

Close to Him

The enormous wealth of love
God has for you compels Him to
shower you with His presence and
draw you close to Him. The fresh
scent that remains after a spring
rain shower is an open invitation
to rest in His mercy and grace.
The flutter of a hummingbird's
wings or the gentle sigh from
a toddler's crib sends a special
message that expresses His gentle
desire to satisfy your heart with
everything good.

Cares of the World

Lord, help me forget the cares of
the world for today; fill my heart
with light as Your blessings fall
upon me and I grow closer to You.
Amen.

What I Seek

One thing I ask of the LORD, this is what I seek: that I may dwell in the house of the LORD all the days of my life, to gaze upon the beauty of the LORD and to seek him in his temple.

PSALM 27:4 NIV

Faith Will Lead You

Read the Word, and it will be
much for your comfort. Search
it and you will grow strong in
the Lord and in the power of His
might. Faith will lead you where
you cannot walk. Reason has never
been a mountain climber.

E. W. KENYON

Joy Ahead

So be truly glad. There is wonderful joy ahead, even though you have to endure many trials for a little while. These trials will show that your faith is genuine. It is being tested as fire tests and purifies gold—though your faith is far more precious than mere gold. So when your faith remains strong through many trials, it will bring you much praise and glory and honor on the day when Jesus Christ is revealed to the whole world.

1 PETER 1:6–7 NLT

Praise the Lord

Praise the LORD. Praise God in his sanctuary; praise him in his mighty heavens. Praise him for his acts of power; praise him for his surpassing greatness. . . . Let everything that has breath praise the LORD. Praise the LORD.

PSALM 150:1–2, 6 NIV

Sleep Peacefully

As you fall asleep, think of just
how much God loves you. Build
your faith by recalling all He
has done for you. Count your
blessings instead of sheep; then
sleep peacefully in your heavenly
Father's protective arms.

Pray Now

It is not a question of praying and asking God to help you; it is taking the grace of God now. We tend to make prayer the preparation for our service, yet it is never that in the Bible. Prayer is the practice of drawing on the grace of God. . . . Pray now; draw on the grace of God in your moment of need.

OSWALD CHAMBERS

Strengthened from Within

When you invite God to fill
your heart and life, you are
strengthened from within. His
strength literally becomes your
strength. You are empowered to
do, to stand, to fight, to conquer.
If Christ is there, you don't need
to reach outside yourself for
strength. Reach inside and find all
you need.

Almighty

If your faith is in experiences,
anything that happens is likely to
upset that faith; but nothing can
ever upset God or the almighty
Reality of Redemption.

OSWALD CHAMBERS

Refreshed

God has given you strength for
your days—even the toughest
ones. He is the source you can
draw on when you feel that your
supply is running low. You don't
have to go at life alone. When you
reach for Him, He's always there,
ready to refresh you.

Spills into Joy

We pray that you'll have the
strength to stick it out over the
long haul—not the grim strength
of gritting your teeth but the glory-
strength God gives. It is strength
that endures the unendurable and
spills over into joy.

COLOSSIANS 1:11 MSG

Thank You, Lord

Even when sin filled every corner
of my life, Father, You did not
despise me. Your mercy turned me
into a new person. May I share
that blessing with those whose
spirits or pocketbooks are needy.
Amen.

Highest Aspirations

Far away, there in the sunshine,
are my highest aspirations. . . .
I can look up and see their beauty,
believe in them, and try to follow
where they lead.

LOUISA MAY ALCOTT

Practical Faith

This is a sane, wholesome, practical working faith: That it is man's business to do the will of God; second, that God Himself takes on the care of that man; and third, that therefore that man ought never to be afraid of anything.

GEORGE MACDONALD

By Grace

For it is by grace you have been
saved, through faith—and this
not from yourselves, it is the gift
of God—not by works, so that no
one can boast.

EPHESIANS 2:8–9 NIV

His Touch

Herein is grace and graciousness!
Herein is love and lovingkindness!
How it opens to us the compassion
of Jesus—so gentle, tender,
considerate! We need never shrink
back from His touch.

CHARLES H. SPURGEON

Indescribable Joy

Although you have not seen him,
you love him; and even though
you do not see him now, you
believe in him and rejoice with an
indescribable and glorious joy, for
you are receiving the outcome of
your faith, the salvation of your
souls.

1 PETER 1:8–9 NRSV

You Will Provide

Lord, thank You for making Your
will clear by calling my heart
to give. I offer my finances and
future to You, knowing that You
will provide for me. Amen.

Peace

The LORD bless thee, and keep thee: the LORD make his face shine upon thee, and be gracious unto thee: the LORD lift up his countenance upon thee, and give thee peace.

NUMBERS 6:24–26 KJV

You Know Me

O LORD, you have searched me and you know me. You know when I sit and when I rise; you perceive my thoughts from afar. You discern my going out and my lying down; you are familiar with all my ways.

PSALM 139:1–3 NIV

His Gift to Us

God cannot believe for us. Faith
is a gift of God—but whether or
not we shall act upon that faith
lies altogether within our own
power. We may or we may not, as
we choose.

A. W. TOZER

Kind and Loving

*How kind and loving You are, O God.
You gave up Your heavenly kingdom
and came to earth for us. When You
viewed my sins, You showed Your
mercy and grace by dying for me.
Thank You for Your love.*

I trusted in thee, O LORD: I said,
Thou art my God. My times are in
thy hand.

PSALM 31:14–15 KJV

Faith Is the Foundation

Works without faith are like
a fish without water: It wants
the element it should live in. A
building without a basis cannot
stand; faith is the foundation, and
every good action is as a stone
laid.

OWEN FELTHAM

Blessing upon Blessing

The heavenly Father welcomes
us with open arms and imparts to
us blessing upon blessing—not
because we are upright, but
because Jesus Christ has clothed
us with His own virtue. The soul
must stand in the sunlight to bear
witness to the sun.

PHILLIPS BROOKS

Lasting Success

True success comes when you're
willing to say, "It's not about me
and all about You, Lord." Then
He is free to take you to a level
that you can only achieve with
His strength and power propelling
you. Then you'll discover lasting
success in Him.

Spread the Gospel

Remind me, Lord, that my task is
to spread the joyful gospel to all,
to believe that You will make my
efforts fruitful, and to never stand
in the way of another's salvation.
Open my heart and show me
where I am needed, and I will trust
the rest to You. Amen.

In Every Circumstance

The light and life of God lives in you; therefore the blessing of truth is always available to you, helping you know and discern what is good and right for your life. Jesus never promised that your pathway would be easy, but He has promised to never leave you. Truth is always with you. And you can call upon Him in every circumstance to light your way.

All of Himself

An infinite God can give all of
Himself to each of His children.
He does not distribute Himself
that each may have a part, but to
each one He gives all of Himself
as fully as if there were no others.

A. W. TOZER

Be Our Strength

Father, hear the prayer we offer,
Not for ease that prayer shall be,
But for strength that we may ever
Live our lives courageously.
Be our strength in
  hours of weakness;
In our wanderings be our guide;
Through endeavor, failure, danger,
Father, be Thou at our side.

LOVE M. WILLIS

Faith + Works

You do right when you offer faith to God; you do right when you offer works. But if you separate the two, then you do wrong. For faith without works is dead.

BERNARD OF CLAIRVAUX

Right Relationship

You never can measure what God
will do through you if you are
rightly related to Jesus Christ.
Keep your relationship right with
Him; then whatever circumstances
you are in and whoever you meet
day by day, He is pouring rivers of
living water through you, and it is
of His mercy that He does not let
you know it.

OSWALD CHAMBERS

Inexhaustible Richness

God's richness is such that He can
totally give Himself to every man,
can be there only for him—and
likewise for a second and third,
for millions and thousands of
millions. That is the mystery of
His infinity and inexhaustible
richness.

LADISLAUS BOROS

Anything Is Possible

No matter how I strive to live in
righteousness, Lord, I will always
fall short of Your standards.
Thank You for making my
perfection possible in the life to
come. By myself, I would certainly
fail. With You, anything is
possible. Amen.

Endless Wonders

As we grow in our capacities to
see and enjoy the delights that
God has placed in our lives, life
becomes a glorious experience of
discovering His endless wonders.
Give thanks for unknown
blessings already on their way.

NATIVE AMERICAN PROVERB

Walk with God

Whatever attributes may compose the character of Deity, every one of them to its fullest extent shall be engaged on our side. God's grace is illustrated and magnified in the poverty and trials of believers. I would rather walk with God in the dark than go alone in the light.

MARY GARDINER BRAINARD

Trust like Jesus

Our Lord never put His trust
in any person. Yet He was never
suspicious, never bitter, and never
lost hope for anyone, because He
put His trust in God first. He
trusted absolutely in what God's
grace could do for others.

OSWALD CHAMBERS

Arms of Faith

Fold the arms of your faith and
wait in quietness until the light
goes up in your darkness. Fold the
arms of your faith, I say, but not of
your action. Think of something
you ought to do and go do it. Heed
not your feelings. Do your work.

GEORGE MACDONALD

Walk in His Light

When Jesus comes into our hearts,
He illumines the Word of God
and shines with all the effulgence
of His glory. Perpetual day is for
those who walk in His light.

CHARLES E. HURLBURT AND T. C. HORTON

For Himself

God's great purpose for the human race [is] that He created us for Himself. This realization of our election by God is the most joyful on earth, and we must learn to rely on this tremendous creative purpose of God.

OSWALD CHAMBERS

New Faith

Lord, when sin causes me to feel
doubt or dullness, You don't toss
me out of Your kingdom but
instead call me to new faith. I need
You to renew me constantly. Make
me new again this day. Amen.

Everywhere

God is infinite in His simplicity
and simple in His infinity.
Therefore He is everywhere
and is everywhere complete.
He is everywhere on account of
His infinity and is everywhere
complete on account of His
simplicity.

MEISTER ECKHART

Trust

Trust in the LORD with all your
heart, and lean not on your own
understanding; in all your ways
acknowledge Him, and He shall
direct your paths.

PROVERBS 3:5–6 NKJV

Thy Wonders

I sing the goodness of the Lord,
That filled the earth with food;
He formed the creatures
  with His word,
And then pronounced them good.
Lord, how Thy wonders
  are displayed,
Where'er I turn my eye:
If I survey the ground I tread,
Or gaze upon the sky!

ISAAC WATTS

Nothing but God

For each of us the time is surely coming when we shall have nothing but God. Health and wealth and friends and hiding places will all be swept away. . . . To the man of pseudo faith that is a terrifying thought, but to real faith it is one of the most comforting thoughts the heart can entertain.

A. W. TOZER

God Governs

I have lived a long time, and the longer I live, the more convincing proof I see of this truth, that God governs in the affairs of men. If a sparrow cannot fall to the ground without His notice, is it probable that an empire can rise without His aid?

BENJAMIN FRANKLIN

Count Your Blessings

Add to your joy by counting your
blessings. He only is the Maker of
all things near and far; He paints
the wayside flower, He lights the
evening star; the wind and waves
obey Him, by Him the birds
are fed; much more to us, His
children, He gives our daily bread.

MATTHIAS CLAUDIUS

A Clean Heart

Create in me a clean heart, O God; and renew a right spirit within me. Cast me not away from thy presence; and take not thy holy spirit from me. Restore unto me the joy of thy salvation; and uphold me with thy free spirit.

PSALM 51:10–12 KJV

Take My Life

How can I repay Your gift of
freedom from sin, Lord? I can't,
so take my life; keep me strong in
You. My life is Yours, Father. May
I honor You all my days. Amen.

The Catch

It's for you I created the universe
[says God]. I love you. There's only
one catch. Like any other gift, the
gift of grace can be yours only if
you'll reach out and take it. Maybe
being able to reach out and take it
is a gift, too.

FREDERICK BUECHNER

Treasure in Nature

If we are children of God, we have
a tremendous treasure in nature
and will realize that it is holy and
sacred. We will see God reaching
out to us in every wind that blows,
every sunrise and sunset, every
cloud in the sky, every flower that
blooms, and every leaf that fades.

OSWALD CHAMBERS

Wherever We Go

God has not made a little universe.
He has made the wide stretches
of space and has put there all the
flaming hosts we see at night, all
the planets, stars, and galaxies.
Wherever we go, let us remind
ourselves that God has made
everything we see. . . . And not
only did God make it all, but He is
present.

FRANCIS A. SCHAEFFER

Help in Trouble

*As I go about my duties, may Your
joy radiate through me. Let Your light
shine in me, Your servant, because of
the good work You have done. I sing
praises and am blessed with Your
strength.*

God is our refuge and strength,
an ever-present help in trouble.
Therefore we will not fear.

PSALM 46:1–2 NIV

Always Within Range

Lord, I wonder how many times
You walked backward, keeping
me in sight and waiting for me to
follow. O Lord, I am so thankful
that You never give up on me and
that I am always within the viewing
range of my Father's eyes.

PAMELA KAYE TRACY

Thanks and Praise

It is right and good that we, for all
things, at all times, and in all places,
give thanks and praise to You, O
God. We worship You, we confess to
You, we praise You, we bless You, we
sing to You, and we give thanks to
You: Maker, Nourisher, Guardian,
Healer, Lord, and Father of all.

LANCELOT ANDREWES

Way to Happiness

If anyone would tell you the
shortest, surest way to happiness
and all perfection, he must tell
you to make it a rule to yourself
to thank and praise God for
everything that happens to you.
For it is certain that whatever
seeming calamity happens to you,
if you thank and praise God for it,
you turn it into a blessing.

WILLIAM LAW

Prayer for Leaders

Father, I ask that You watch over
my spiritual leaders today and
all the days to come. Wherever
possible, make their loads lighter;
where that is impossible, make
their shoulders strong. Be with
them and assure them that their
work is not in vain. Amen.

His Peace

Calm me, O Lord,
   as you stilled the storm,
Still me, O Lord,
   keep me from harm.
Let all the tumult within me cease,
Enfold me, Lord, in your peace.

CELTIC TRADITIONAL

Waiting. . .

How exciting to know that what
you've asked God for is on its way.
As God works behind the scenes
to bring about everything you're
waiting for, your faith is at work
preparing for the arrival of His
blessing.

Your Confidence

When you lie down, you will not
be afraid; when you lie down, your
sleep will be sweet. Have no fear of
sudden disaster or of the ruin that
overtakes the wicked, for the LORD
will be your confidence and will
keep your foot from being snared.

PROVERBS 3:24–26 NIV

Faith and Works

Faith and works are as necessary
to our spiritual life as Christians
as soul and body are to our lives
as men; for faith is the soul of
religion and works of the body.

CHARLES CALEB COLTON

Share the Light

The smile on your face is the light in the window that tells people you're at home. Happiness is a sunbeam. . . . When it strikes a kindred heart, like the converged lights upon a mirror, it reflects itself with redoubled brightness. It is not perfected until it is shared.

JANE PORTER

Godly Leaders

Touch those godly leaders in my
life who have pointed me to You.
When they face discouragement,
lift them up. Let my lips be quick
to offer uplifting words. Amen.

God's Handwriting

Never lose an opportunity
of seeing anything that is
beautiful; for beauty is God's
handwriting—a wayside
sacrament. Welcome it in every
fair face, in every fair sky, in every
fair flower, and thank God for it as
a cup of blessing.

RALPH WALDO EMERSON

Fear or Faith

Fear imprisons, faith liberates;
fear paralyzes, faith empowers; fear
disheartens, faith encourages; fear
sickens, faith heals; fear makes
useless, faith makes serviceable—
and, most of all, fear puts
hopelessness at the heart of life,
while faith rejoices in its God.

HARRY EMERSON FOSDICK

Glad Praises

We praise Thee, O God,
   our Redeemer, Creator,
In grateful devotion
   our tribute we bring;
We lay it before Thee,
   we kneel and adore Thee,
We bless Thy holy Name,
   glad praises we sing.

JULIA BUCKLEY CADY CORY

Never Changing

When all else is gone, God is left,
and nothing changes Him. Let the
thankful heart sweep through the
day, and, as the magnet finds the
iron, so it will find in every hour
some heavenly blessing; only the
iron in God's hand is gold.

HENRY WARD BEECHER

Key to Happiness

The key to happiness belongs to everyone on earth who recognizes simple things as treasures of great worth. It is impossible to enjoy idling thoroughly unless one has plenty of work to do.

JEROME K. JEROME

A Good Witness

Remind me that my view of time is not the same as Yours. I receive Your blessings in Your good time, and the grace with which I wait for them shows others a lot about me—and about You. Make me a good witness, Father. Amen.

Grow in Wisdom

The Holy Spirit dwells within you,
reading to give you the wisdom
you need to make good choices
for your life. If you're listening,
you will hear Him; but He is a
gentleman. He won't shout or
force you to hear what He has to
say. The more you trust His lead,
the more you will grow in wisdom.

The Lord Is Good

Enter into his gates with
thanksgiving, and into his courts
with praise: be thankful unto him,
and bless his name. For the LORD
is good; his mercy is everlasting;
and his truth endureth to all
generations.

PSALM 100:4–5 KJV

Faith with Works

Faith without works is like a bird without wings; though she may hop about on earth, she will never fly to heaven. But when both are joined together, then doth the soul mount up to her eternal rest.

FRANCIS BEAUMONT

Child of God

Sometimes you wonder if what you do really matters—it does. God will not forget you. He will be your companion day after day. And He will reward you one day in front of everyone. Labor on, child of God. Sleep well at night knowing that God is pleased with you.

Senior Partner

God makes us covenant partners
in the working out of His purposes
in the world, and yet we are not
equal partners. God is the senior
partner and must therefore be
approached in awe and reverence.

DONALD G. BLOESCH

Wisdom of Faith

He who trusts in the Lord has a
diploma for wisdom granted by
inspiration: Happy is he now, and
happier shall he be above. Lord,
teach me the wisdom of faith.
Faith is the radar that sees through
the fog the reality of things at
a distance that the human eye
cannot see.

CORRIE TEN BOOM

Relying upon God

I have often wished that I
was a more decent man. . . .
Nevertheless, amid the greatest
difficulties of my administration,
when I could not see any other
resort, I would place my whole
reliance upon God.

ABRAHAM LINCOLN

WHISPERS OF
Faith

Where Angels Sing

There is singing up in heaven such
as we have never known, where the
angels sing the praises of the Lamb
upon the throne; their sweet harps
are always tuneful and their voices
always clear. O, that we might be
more like them as we serve the
Master here.

JOHNSON OATMAN JR.

Advocate with God

There is nothing that makes us
love a man so much as praying for
him. . . . By considering yourself
as an advocate with God for your
neighbors and acquaintances, you
would never find it hard to be at
peace with them yourself.

WILLIAM LAW

Benefit of Patience

I want to learn the benefit of
patience, Lord, without the
struggles. Change my heart to
wait on You quietly and without
complaint, so that I will be ready
for Your coming. Amen.

Anxiety Cure

Need a cure for anxiety? Start
praying. As you trust that God
has your best interests at heart,
no matter what situation you face,
His peace can replace concern.
God says there's nothing you need
to worry about. Just put all your
troubles in His hands. . . .

PAMELA McQUADE

Resist the Devil

Discipline yourselves; keep alert.
Like a roaring lion your adversary
the devil prowls around, looking
for someone to devour. Resist
him, steadfast in your faith, for
you know that your brothers and
sisters throughout the world are
undergoing the same kinds of
suffering.

1 PETER 5:8–9 NRSV

Pay Our Praises

The sun. . . .in its full glory, either
at rising or setting—this, and
many other like blessings we enjoy
daily; and for the most of them,
because they are so common, most
men forget to pay their praises.
But let not us.

IZAAK WALTON

Don't Wear Out

After a long, frustrating day at work, whether we use our muscles or our brains on the job, we all know what it is to be worn out. But we can wear out spiritually, too. Jesus tells us to come to Him when weariness floods our souls. When we drink deeply at His well, the energy will begin to flow.

Casting Cares

Forgive me, Father. Time and
again I've been so stressed that I
wanted to give up on life. I tried so
hard to get through each day, but I
never bothered to give my worries
to You. I've fought through each
task and brought grief to others by
trying to struggle alone; from now
on, I'm casting my cares on You!

RACHEL QUILLIN

Humble and Contrite
in Spirit

"Has not my hand made all these things, and so they came into being?" declares the LORD. "This is the one I esteem: he who is humble and contrite in spirit, and trembles at my word."

ISAIAH 66:2 NIV

Expect Everything

We should act with as much energy as those who expect everything from themselves, and we should pray with as much earnestness as those who expect everything from God.

CHARLES CALEB COLTON

Our Hope

Praise awaits you, O God. . . .
You answer us with awesome deeds
of righteousness, O God our
Savior, the hope of all the ends of
the earth and of the farthest seas.

PSALM 65:1, 5 NIV

A Leap of the Heart

Prayer is an upward leap of the
heart, an untroubled glance toward
heaven, a cry of gratitude and love
which I utter from the depths of
sorrow as well as from the heights
of joy. It has supernatural grandeur
that expands the soul and unites it
with God.

THÉRÈSE OF LISIEUX

Your Will and Guidance

Open my mind and heart to Your
will and guidance; help me live as
a citizen of a righteous nation; put
out the forest fire of war. Bring
lasting peace and justice, Lord,
to the world You love so much.
Amen.

Love to Pray

Love to pray—feel often during
the day the need for prayer,
and take trouble to pray. Prayer
enlarges the heart until it is
capable of containing God's gift of
Himself.

MOTHER TERESA

Special

How can I doubt my worth in Your
eyes, Father? You know the number
of hairs on my head. You created
me, and You said that Your creation
is very good. When I'm tempted
to get down on myself, remind me
that I am special to You, and there's
no one just like me.

RACHEL QUILLIN

Face-to-Face

I had walked life's path
  with an easy tread,
Had followed where
  comfort and pleasure led;
And then one day in a quiet place
I met the Master, face-to-face.

UNKNOWN

Reaching Out

When trials come your way, God
will [draw you close to His heart].
If life is always going smoothly,
comfort is meaningless; but when
you're in the midst of trouble,
He comes alongside with tender
love that overflows your trials and
reaches out to others.

PAMELA MCQUADE

Tiny Heart

In comparison with this big world, the human heart is only a small thing. Though the world is so large, it is utterly unable to satisfy this tiny heart. Our ever-growing soul and its capacities can be satisfied only in the infinite God.

SADHU SUNDAR SINGH

Gladness and Joy

Therefore the redeemed of the
LORD shall return, and come with
singing unto Zion; and everlasting
joy shall be upon their head: they
shall obtain gladness and joy; and
sorrow and mourning shall flee
away.

ISAIAH 51:11 KJV

His Kingdom

Thank You for Your promise that
as I obey, You'll make me part of
a kingdom of priests in a holy
nation. Your kingdom, Father, is
better than this world could ever
be. I want to be an active part of it.
Amen.

Contentment

It's a fast-paced world where everyone wants to get ahead, Father. Sometimes contentment is frowned upon. Some folks think of it as laziness or lack of motivation. But I know that if I am in the center of Your will, I'll be content. That's the only true contentment there is.

RACHEL QUILLIN

Assurance

Take comfort in the fact that your
prayer partner, your friend and
comrade, is God Himself. You can
take any request to Him with the
assurance that He will hear you.
As you do, be sure to thank Him
for His help.

REBECCA CURRINGTON AND PATRICIA MITCHELL

Forever Be Praise

With voices united our praises we
   offer,
To Thee, great Jehovah, glad
   anthems we raise.
Thy strong arm will guide us, our
   God is beside us,
To Thee, our great Redeemer,
   forever be praise.

JULIA BUCKLEY CADY CORY

Faith

When outward strength is broken,
faith rests on the promises. In the
midst of sorrow, faith draws the sting
out of every trouble and takes out
the bitterness from every affliction.

ROBERT CECIL

God's Methods

God's methods don't change because
we are so noisy and busy. He is
longing for your attention, your
individual and full attention. . . .
He will wait and wait until you
finally sit in silence and listen.

CHARLES SWINDOLL

Spiritual Cobwebs

Today, allow [God] to search your
heart. Ask Him to dig deep. Are
there cobwebs that need to be
swept out? Things hidden that
should be revealed? Let God wash
away your anxieties, replacing
them with His exceeding great joy!

JANICE HANNA

The Only Rock

Often my foundation is undependable, and it can send my life tumbling down after one bad storm. Teach me to ground my life on You, Lord, the only Rock who will stand forever against any storm. Amen.

A Summer's Day

Rest is not idleness, and to lie
sometimes on the grass under trees
on a summer's day, listening to the
murmur of the water, or watching
the clouds float across the sky, is
by no means a waste of time.

SIR JOHN LUBBOCK

Confidence

There is no calm deeper than
that which succeeds a storm.
Our confidence must not be in
what we have done nor in what we
have resolved to do, but entirely
in what the Lord will do. Pure and
simple, faith not lived every day is
not faith, it is facade.

UNKNOWN

Excellent or Praiseworthy

Whatever is true, whatever is
noble, whatever is right, whatever
is pure, whatever is lovely, whatever
is admirable—if anything is
excellent or praiseworthy—think
about such things.

PHILIPPIANS 4:8 NIV

Pure Delight

You have to know Jesus to delight
in His presence, just as you cannot
enjoy a friend until you come
to know each other and enjoy
companionship. But knowing
and loving God brings us, His
children, joy in His presence
and the prospect of undefined
pleasures at His side. Are you
prepared to share those joys with
Jesus for eternity?

PAMELA MCQUADE

United In Prayer

I have learned a great deal
about prayer, praying for other
people when the need arises,
spontaneously and
immediately. . . .We can share
with each other without being
threatened by each other's
differences because we know that
we are united by Christ, and this
union is a union of love and not
fear.

MADELEINE L'ENGLE

Beautiful

For the Creator, every nuance,
every brushstroke, every indention
in the clay has meaning. God
created you—with intention and
purpose. You are His work of art.
In His eyes, you are beautiful in
every way, inside and out.

REBECCA CURRINGTON AND PATRICIA MITCHELL

Obedience

I know I can't obey You all on my
own, Lord. When I try, I just get
tied up in all the good I want to
do. Make my heart all Yours, and
I will no longer struggle with sin.
When my soul prospers, surely my
life will be blessed. Amen.

Joy!

Want to know the secret of
walking in the fullness of joy?
Draw near to the Lord. Allow His
Spirit to fill you daily. Let Him
whisper sweet nothings in your ear
and woo you with His love. The
Spirit of God is your Comforter,
your Friend. He fills you to
overflowing. Watch the joy flow!

JANICE HANNA

I Believe It

Your faith would lose its glory if
it rested on anything discernible
by the carnal eye. Faith takes
God without any ifs. If God says
anything, faith says, "I believe it";
faith says "Amen" to it.

D. L. MOODY

Amazing Riches

Sometimes I find myself worrying
about my financial situation. I
have a tendency to forget that
my Father owns the cattle on a
thousand hills—and everything
else, too. I know You'll take care of
me, Lord. Amen.

RACHEL QUILLIN

Pass It On

Has a faithful Bible teacher
opened the Word to you? Avoid
leaving without appreciating the
impact of that teaching on your
thoughts and deeds. Support the
person who brought you God's
message—and somehow, pass it on
to another who needs a blessing
today.

Home

We can have faith in God's
perfection. He has never failed His
people yet, though they have often
been false. Trust in Him today. As
He led His people to the Promised
Land, He'll lead you home to
Himself.

PAMELA MCQUADE

God's Promise

God has said, "Never will I leave
you; never will I forsake you." So
we say with confidence, "The Lord
is my helper; I will not be afraid.
What can man do to me?"

HEBREWS 13:5–6 NIV

Enough!

Nothing can separate you from
His love, absolutely nothing....
God is enough for time, and God
is enough for eternity. God is
enough!

HANNAH WHITALL SMITH

Belonging

We all want to belong. . . .
Unfortunately, our culture places
value on so many things that have
no lasting meaning—where we
live, how we dress. . . . Comfort
yourself with the truth that God
values you for who you really are
deep inside, nothing more, nothing
less. You are His magnificent
creation. . . . You belong to Him.

REBECCA CURRINGTON AND PATRICIA MITCHELL

Enduring Hardship

Help me see the value of patiently enduring hardship. I look forward with joy to eternity with You. Strengthen me, Lord, to be patient until that day. Amen.

A Temple

The soul is a temple, and God
is silently building it by night
and by day. Precious thoughts
are building it, unselfish love is
building it; all-penetrating faith is
building it.

HENRY WARD BEECHER

Bearing Fruit

A Christian who doesn't spend
much time with the Savior bears
little fruit. But a believer who
taps into Him every day, spending
time talking and listening to
Him, through prayer and the
Word, begins to burgeon with it.
Opportunities to reach out will
come, and the fruit will become
heavier all the time.

All-Sufficient Grace

If then yours is a much-tried path,
rejoice in it because you will better
show forth the all-sufficient grace
of God. Great faith is not the
faith that walks always in the light
and knows no darkness, but the
faith that perseveres in spite of
God's seeming silences.

FATHER ANDREW

Saving Faith

Faith is not something you commit
to once then don't think about
again. Instead it's something that
alerts you every day to possibilities
and opportunities. . . .
Soon you will stop worrying about
what's around the next corner.
You'll know with certainty that
the two of you can handle any
eventuality.

Best Friends

True friendship with God. . .means being so intimately in touch with God that you never even need to ask Him to show you His will. You are God's will. And all of your seemingly commonsense decisions are actually His will for you, unless you sense a check in your spirit.

OSWALD CHAMBERS

Be Generous

Father, today I pray for those who
are struggling with poverty in my
own community and throughout
the world. Help me be generous
with both my donations and my
efforts to help those in need.
Amen.

Chosen People

Therefore, as God's chosen people,
holy and dearly loved, clothe
yourselves with compassion,
kindness, humility, gentleness and
patience. . . . Forgive as the Lord
forgave you.

COLOSSIANS 3:12–13 NIV

The Hand of God

Nothing touches my life that hasn't first passed through the hand of God. He knows what is best for me. I will trust His hand in my life, believing that He sees how all things work together. Summer afternoon—summer afternoon; to me those have always been the two most beautiful words in the English language.

HENRY JAMES

God's Workmanship

A tried saint, like a well-cut diamond, glitters much in the King's crown. We are God's workmanship, in whom He will be glorified by our afflictions. He who gave Himself for us in the depths of woe and death does not withdraw the grant now that He is enthroned in the highest heavens. Before me, even as behind, God is, and all is well.

JOHN GREENLEAF WHITTIER

A New Awareness

You've probably heard it before—
seeing is not believing; believing
is seeing. It's more than a twist on
a phrase. Your faith opens up to a
new awareness of life around you.
It enables you to see more from
God's point of view. It reminds
you that life is not just about the
everyday realities but also mystery
and possibilities. When you believe,
you live according to a whole other
reality with sights and sounds
unimaginable to faithless eyes.

Your Defender

If you've been hurt by someone
you trusted, choose to release
that person today. Let it go. God
is your defender. He's got your
back. Take refuge in Him. And
remember, praising Him—even in
the storm—will shift your focus
back where it belongs. Praise the
Lord! He is our defense!

Guide You Always

The LORD will guide you always;
he will satisfy your needs in a
sun-scorched land. . . . You will be
like a well-watered garden, like a
spring whose waters never fail.

ISAIAH 58:11 NIV

Obey His Will

Is there something you could do that
God would refuse to help you with?
No, not as long as you're tapped in
to Him and seeking to obey His
will. "And this same God who takes
care of me will supply all your needs
from his glorious riches, which have
been given to us in Christ Jesus"
(Philippians 4:19 NLT).

Rough Road

Thank God, then, if you have
been led by a rough road. It is
this which has given you your
experience of God's greatness and
loving-kindness. It is faith that
brings power, not merely praying
and weeping and struggling, but
believing, daring to believe the
written Word with or without
feeling.

CATHERINE BOOTH

Natural Laws

Science has sometimes been
said to be opposed to faith
and inconsistent with it. But
all science, in fact, rests on a
basis of faith, for it assumes the
permanence and uniformity of
natural laws—a thing which can
never be demonstrated.

TRYON EDWARDS

Power to Obey

Your heavenly Father will never
give you a command that is not
accompanied by ample power
to obey it. And joys and tears
alike are sent to give the soul fit
nourishment. As comes to me or
cloud or sun, Father! Thy will, not
mine, be done.

SARAH FLOWER ADAMS

All the Future

How could I be anything but quite
happy if I believed always that all
the past is forgiven, and all the
present furnished with power, and
all the future bright with hope.

JAMES SMETHAM

Regard for the Poor

I know that You have a special
regard for the poor. Be their
comfort, their hope for the future,
and the one constant presence
they can count on. Amen.

Not in Vain

If I can stop one heart from
   breaking,
I shall not live in vain:
If I can ease one life the aching,
Or cool one pain,
Or help one fainting robin
Unto his nest again,
I shall not live in vain.

EMILY DICKINSON

God's Grace Saves

We can't save anyone. No one comes to God because we do all the right things, say all the right words, or give them books by the best apologists. All those things may help, of course, but no one comes to God because another has witnessed "perfectly." What does save people is God's grace.

Man's Weakness

All providences are doors to
trial. Men have drowned in seas
of prosperity as well as in rivers
of affliction. Real, true faith is
man's weakness leaning on God's
strength.

D. L. MOODY

All Blessings

Faith is the root of all blessings. Believe, and you shall be saved; believe, and your needs must be satisfied; believe, and you cannot but be comforted and happy.

JEREMY TAYLOR

Lavish Love

God does not give His love in
dribs and drabs. . . . God's love lets
loose in our lives. Nothing is too
good for His obedient children.
Praise God that He loves you that
much!

A Willing Heart

Lord, I know that in the center of
Your will are peace, joy, and many
other rich blessings. I'd like to
experience all these things, but the
trouble I seem to have is figuring
out what Your will is for me.
Please help me be attentive when
You speak, and give me a heart
willing to be used by you.

RACHEL QUILLIN

Go in Confidence

He comforts you by opening His arms to you, inviting you to talk to Him about your feelings and the depth of your emotions. Even more, He promises He will listen. Go to Him in confidence, even if you're not sure what to say. He is listening to you.

REBECCA CURRINGTON AND PATRICIA MITCHELL

Move Forward with Joy

We can move forward with joy
leading the way when we realize
that God is the Giver of the
seasons. He designed them and
showers us with blessings as we
move through each one, even the
tough ones! . . . Change is always
just around the bend. Oh, the joy
of knowing that the hard times
won't last.

JANICE HANNA

Perfect in Faith

The man is perfect in faith who
can come to God in the utter
dearth of his feelings and desires,
without a glow or an inspiration,
with the weight of low thoughts,
failures, neglects, and wandering
forgetfulness, and say to Him,
"Thou art my refuge."

GEORGE MACDONALD

Anywhere

I'll go anywhere, my Savior,
If Thou wilt make it clear,
I will tell salvation's story
To lost ones far and near.
Anywhere, my Savior,
Anywhere with Thee,
Anywhere and ev'rywhere,
As Thou leadest me.

JOHN R. CLEMENTS

Flow

As your faith is strengthened, you
will find that there is no longer the
need to have a sense of control,
that things will flow as they will,
and that you will flow with them,
to your great delight and benefit.

EMMANUEL TENEY

Mustard Seed Faith

"If you have faith as small as a mustard seed, you can say to this mountain, 'Move from here to there,' and it will move. Nothing will be impossible for you."

MATTHEW 17:20–21 NIV

To Reveal Himself

The Lord's chief desire is to reveal
Himself to you, and in order for
Him to do that, He gives you
abundant grace. The Lord gives
you the experience of enjoying His
presence. He touches you, and His
touch is so delightful that, more
than ever, you are drawn inwardly
to Him.

MADAME JEANNE GUYON

Promises Kept

Our faithful Lord provides for all His created beings. . . . How could He satisfy the needs of the smallest birds and beasts yet forget His human child? God is always faithful. Though we fail, He will not. He cannot forget His promises of love and will never forget to provide for your every need.

PAMELA MCQUADE

Glory of God

The heavens declare the glory of
God; the skies proclaim the work
of his hands. Day after day they
pour forth speech; night after
night they display knowledge.

PSALM 19:1–2 NIV

Wall of Fire

We do not know what we might
have been if God's gracious
protection had not been like a wall
of fire around us, as it still is, for
the Lord continues to deliver all
those who put their trust in Him.
Faith is a higher faculty than
reason.

PHILIP JAMES BAILEY

A Cheerful Heart

The real secret of happiness is not what you give or what you receive; it's what you share. Since God has given me a cheerful heart, He will forgive me for serving Him cheerfully.

FRANZ JOSEF HAYDN

A Map for Me

Your Word never fails me. It is
like a map for me to find my way.
I open it and marvel at all its
wisdom. Thank You for providing
these scriptures so I can find
direction in my life.

Rejoice

Do not rejoice in earthly reality;
rejoice in Christ, rejoice in His
word, rejoice in His law. . . . There
will be peace and tranquility in
the Christian heart, but only as
long as our faith is watchful; if,
however, our faith sleeps, we are in
danger.

AUGUSTINE OF HIPPO

Resting in the Joy

Jesus, I am resting, resting in the
joy of what Thou art;
I am finding out the greatness of
Thy loving heart.
Thou hast bid me gaze upon Thee,
and Thy beauty fills my soul,
For by Thy transforming power,
Thou hast made me whole.

JEAN SOPHIA PIGOTT

Blessed Indeed

As I grow in faith, remind me of
my need for You, the source of my
spiritual riches. Without You, I am
poor, yet You offer me the riches
of heaven. I am blessed indeed.
Amen.

God-Pleaser

Instead of chasing after the things this world can offer, which are nothing more than wind, chase after God. Be a God-pleaser. Store up His treasures. He is the Giver of all things and will make sure you have all you need. . .and more. What joy in finding that treasure!

JANICE HANNA

Confidence

I suggest that we go forward with
great confidence, for although
every day will bring dangers,
every day will also witness divine
deliverances. Faith is a living and
unshakable confidence, a belief in
the grace of God so assured that a
man would die a thousand deaths
for its sake.

MARTIN LUTHER

Through the Rivers

Tried faith brings experience.
You could not have believed your
own weakness had you not been
compelled to pass through the rivers;
and you would never have known
God's strength had you not been
supported amid the water-floods.
Faith expects from God what is
beyond all expectation.

ANDREW MURRAY

Unchangeable

As you take your hurt, your
embarrassment, your shame
to God, don't forget His
unchangeable love for you. He has
promised you the gift of His Holy
Spirit to give you strength and
comfort, and you should expect no
less. He will never fail you.

REBECCA CURRINGTON AND PATRICIA MITCHELL

Gentle Peace

Thank You, Lord, for this
opportunity to bask in the peace
that You offer. . . . I am reminded
how Your presence in my life
soothes even in the midst of chaos.
I'm glad to have Your peace!

RACHEL QUILLIN

A Friend

Words cannot express the joy
which a friend imparts; they only
can know who have experienced.
A friend is dearer than the light of
heaven, for it would be better for
us that the sun were extinguished
than that we should be without
friends.

JOHN CHRYSOSTOM

Still with God

Knowing God is not about what
we do, but about whom we love.
Our good works mean little if we
disconnect from Him. Spend time
being still with God today, and a
deepened knowledge of Him will
be your blessing.

PAMELA MCQUADE

Paradox of Faith

The greatness of God rouses
fear within us, but His goodness
encourages us not to be afraid of
Him. To fear and not be afraid—
that is the paradox of faith.

A. W. TOZER

God Will Provide

We've all had tasks that looked
easy at the onset, but later
threatened to scuttle our resolve.
We wonder if it's worth it to
hang on. But when we do, we
find that the reward of the task
accomplished is even sweeter. Are
you wondering if you can finish
the task God has assigned for you?
Don't give up. Your faithfulness to
God's purposes holds the promise
of great reward. Ask God to help
you faithfully carry on until the
job is done.

Lovely Days

Our Creator would never have
made such lovely days and have
given us the deep hearts to enjoy
them, above and beyond all
thought, unless we were meant to
be immortal.

NATHANIEL HAWTHORNE

Little Things

It's the little things that make up
the richest part of the tapestry of
our lives. From God, great and
small, rich and poor, draw living
water from a living spring, and
those who serve Him freely and
gladly will receive grace answering
to grace.

THOMAS À KEMPIS

God at Work

If someone has repeatedly hurt you, ask the Lord to give you wisdom regarding the relationship; then ask Him to give you the capacity to forgive even when it seems impossible. Surely joy will rise up in your soul as you watch God at work.

JANICE HANNA

Faith, Hope, Love

Faith makes all things possible.
Hope makes all things bright.
Love makes all things easy.

AUGUSTINE

Freedom

God offers you the priceless
freedom of being able to live
each day of your life free from
the chains of guilt, despair, and
hopelessness. He has opened to
you the door to freedom as His
Spirit directs you along the path
He has laid out for you, a path
leading to genuine happiness and
lasting liberty.

REBECCA CURRINGTON AND PATRICIA MITCHELL

Faith Perseveres

Great faith is not the faith that
walks always in the light and
knows no darkness, but the faith
that perseveres in spite of God's
seeming silences.

FATHER ANDREW

Continual Praise

Lord, may the life I live be a
continual sacrifice of praise to
You. You, who have done so much
for me, ask only that I give my life
wholly to You. How can I refuse?
Let what others see in me be cause
for them to glorify You, too.

RACHEL QUILLIN

Perfect Love

Want to fully experience God's
perfect love? Then obey Him.
When we walk the way Jesus did,
we obey the Father. Instead of
taking the glory for ourselves, we lift
up the One who really deserves it.

More Faith

He makes your experience to be
suitable to bring out some point
of His glory, which could not
be brought out otherwise. What
we have done, as believers, in
glorifying God is far, far short of
His due. Think, my dear brother
or sister, what the Lord has done
for you. The secret behind getting
more faith is to get to know God
more.

LESTER SUMRALL

Fervent Faith

God's best gifts, like valuable
jewels, are kept under lock and key,
and those who want them must,
with fervent faith, importunately
ask for them; for God is a
rewarder of them that diligently
seek Him.

D. L. MOODY

Ever More Faithful

Only as God's Spirit works in our
heart will our whole being become
ever more faithful. God works in
us day by day, perfecting our love.
Ask Him to help you love Him
today.

PAMELA MCQUADE

Paradise

Flowers are God's thoughts of
beauty, taking form to gladden
mortal gaze; bright gems of earth,
in which, perchance, we see what
Eden was—what Paradise may be!

WILLIAM WILBERFORCE

WHISPERS OF
Faith

Seasons

God has seasons in our lives. . . .
He is creating something you'll
enjoy in the future. You may not
understand it today, but a month
or a year later, you'll experience
the benefits of the new growth He
was watering.

TONI SORTOR AND PAMELA McQUADE

The Impossible

God is a God of the impossible.
And He wants us to ask, even
when we're facing insurmountable
obstacles. In fact, He wants us to
know that only He can perform
miracles. Our job? We're called
to trust Him. Then, when those
impossible situations turn around,
our "joy tank" will be completely
filled to overflowing!

JANICE HANNA

His Control

The weather is not ours to control, but God's. We need to give thanks for the daily blessings God offers us—rain that keeps wells and reservoirs filled or sunshine for a special outing. When the weather doesn't go "our way," we can still thank God that He's in control.

God Is Faithful

There hath no temptation taken you
but such as is common to man: but
God is faithful, who will not suffer
you to be tempted above that ye are
able; but will with the temptation
also make a way to escape, that ye
may be able to bear it.

1 CORINTHIANS 10:13 KJV

Heaven, Earth, and Sea

My hope is in You, my God,
my help and strength, You who
created the heaven, the earth, the
sea, and everything. How grand is
the way the earth rotates and tilts
at Your command. I marvel at how
You decided the count of stars and
even know their names!

The Lord Reigns

The LORD reigns forever. . . .
He will govern the peoples with
justice. Those who know your
name will trust in you, for you,
LORD, have never forsaken those
who seek you.

PSALM 9:7–8, 10 NIV

Peace and Joy

God came to us because God
wanted to join us on the road, to
listen to our stories, and to help
us realize that we are not walking
in circles but moving toward the
house of peace and joy.

THOMAS MERTON

Just Be

Don't get so busy that you forget
to simply *be*. Sometimes the best
way to stop being overwhelmed by
life is to simply step back, take a
day. . .or an hour. . .or a moment,
and notice all that God is doing in
your life.

ELLYN SANNA

Rejoice in the Lord

Light is sown for the righteous,
and gladness for the upright in
heart. Rejoice in the LORD, ye
righteous; and give thanks at the
remembrance of his holiness.

PSALM 97:11–12 KJV

Part of God's Burden

A burden, even a small one,
when carried alone and in
isolation, can destroy us; but a
burden when carried as part of
God's burden can lead us to new
life. That is the great mystery of
our faith.

HENRI NOUWEN

Enduring Faithfulness

God won't abandon you. He won't walk away. His faithfulness reaches farther than you can see or even imagine. It's difficult to take in that kind of faithfulness when you live in a world full of disappointments. But if you can get quiet enough inside to sense God's never-changing presence and His steadfast commitment to you, you can survive the disappointments of this life so much more bravely.

The One. . .

Your heart is beating with God's love; open it to others. He has entrusted you with gifts and talents; use them for His service. He goes before you each step of the way; walk in faith. Take courage. Step out into the unknown with the One who knows all.

ELLYN SANNA

His Blessed Will

God is our Father, and He loves
us and knows what is best. His
will is the very most blessed thing
that can come to us under any
circumstance.

HANNAH WHITALL SMITH

Depending on God

We're depending on GOD; he's everything we need. What's more, our hearts brim with joy since we've taken for our own his holy name. Love us, GOD, with all you've got—that's what we're depending on.

PSALM 33:20–22 MSG

True Contentment

If you yearn for the fulfillment
of your dreams and desires, bring
them to the One who knows all
about needs, desires, longings,
yearnings—and miracles. Trust
[God] to draw from your dreams
the pleasure of godly fulfillment
and the satisfaction of true
contentment.

REBECCA CURRINGTON AND PATRICIA MITCHELL

Think to Pray

It is a grand thing to be driven
to think; it is a grander thing to
be driven to pray through having
been made to think. What is faith,
unless it is to believe what you do
not see?

AUGUSTINE

His Heart

Every breath we breathe comes
from God. Every step we take is a
gift from our Creator. We can do
nothing apart from Him. In the
same sense, every joy, every sorrow
. . .God goes through each one
with us. His heart is for us.

JANICE HANNA

A Work in Me

Dear God, I'm a far cry from perfect, but I'm confident in the knowledge that You love me just as I am. You are the One who has begun a work in me, and You will be faithful to complete what has been started. What a thrill to know that You'll make me what You want me to be.

RACHEL QUILLIN

Wonderful Future

Each day can be the beginning of
a wonderful future. "It is good to
praise the LORD and make music
to your name, O Most High, to
proclaim your love in the morning
and your faithfulness at night"
(Psalm 92:1–2 NIV).

Offer Thanks

God wants you to bring to Him
your cries of pain, but He also
invites you to offer Him your
thanks for the good things
happening in your life. . . .
Be thankful, because God is
present with you—loving and
comforting you—every moment
of every day.

REBECCA CURRINGTON AND PATRICIA MITCHELL

Your Body

The work is great, Lord. Whenever
I am tempted to throw up my
hands in defeat, remind me that
I am part of Your Body. Together
we plant the seeds; You will send
the rain and ensure the harvest.
Amen.

Bags of Mercy

Christ Jesus has bags of mercy
that have never even been opened.
That is why the Bible says He has
goodness laid up. . . . Who knows
what will happen if He opens just
one more of these bags?

JOHN BUNYAN

New Mercies

Oh, what joy rises in our souls
as we realize that God's love and
mercy are new every morning!
Each day is a fresh start, a new
chance. Grace washes over us
afresh, like the morning dew.
Great is His faithfulness!

JANICE HANNA

Unfailing Security

God has given us His promises in
order to provide sure footing in
a tumultuous world. He knew we
wouldn't be helped by promises filled
with ambiguity and double-talk, so
He gives it to us straight. . . . Placing
your hope in Him is a no-risk
proposition, because He will never
fail you.

REBECCA CURRINGTON AND PATRICIA MITCHELL

You Are Special

Stand outside this evening. Look
at the stars. Know that you are
special and loved by the One who
created them. God wants nothing
from us except our needs, and
these furnish Him with room
to display His bounty when He
supplies them freely. . . . Not what
I have, but what I do not have, is
the first point of contact between
my soul and God.

CHARLES H. SPURGEON

Whole Faith

Never, never pin your whole faith
on any human being: not if he is
the best and wisest in the whole
world. There are lots of nice things
you can do with sand, but do not
try building a house on it.

C. S. LEWIS

Our Best Friend

Jesus! What a friend for sinners!
Jesus! Lover of my soul;
Friends may fail me,
    foes assail me,
He, my Savior, makes me whole.

J. WILBUR CHAPMAN

No Worries

As you look back on the journey
you've traveled—recall the times
you placed hope and confidence
in God. The outcome might not
have been exactly as you imagined,
but God is always faithful to bring
you through. Count each blessing
He's given you along the way and
consider them stepping stones to a
higher level of trust.

On Loan

I can't earn faith; I can only
borrow it. My faith is on loan from
You, [Lord]. It's mine to cultivate
and grow and enjoy, but it's Your
seed, not mine, and You give it to
me out of love, not as a reward for
anything I've done or not done in
my life.

TONI SORTOR

Justified through Faith

Therefore, since we have been justified through faith, we have peace with God through our Lord Jesus Christ, through whom we have gained access by faith into this grace in which we now stand. And we rejoice in the hope of the glory of God.

ROMANS 5:1–2 NIV

In a Godly Manner

Make me strong when I am weak;
give me courage when I am afraid.
If reproach comes to me, teach
me how to deal with it in a godly
manner, Lord, for the sake of Your
glory. Amen.

Celebrate!

Today, the Lord wants you to reach down into His well of salvation and, with great joy, draw up the bucket. Remember how He saved you? Delivered you? Remember His grace? Is your bucket filled to the brim? If so, then that's something to celebrate!

JANICE HANNA

God's Ways

Man's ways are variable, but God's ways are everlasting. Take up your own daily cross; it is the burden best suited for your shoulder and will prove most effective to make you perfect in every good word and work to the glory of God.

Take Comfort

God's healing sometimes happens overnight, but most often it takes time. Take comfort in knowing that each day in some small way, He is bringing you through, giving you strength, creating for you a future based on His love rather than your past.

REBECCA CURRINGTON AND PATRICIA MITCHELL

Gaining Faith

While my faith is small and puny,
Yours is perfect and mighty,
[Lord]. The life I am living right
now is not the result of my faith
in You but of Your faith in me.
Thank You for Your sacrifice that
saves me and makes me whole.

TONI SORTOR

Glorious Promises

The most glorious promises of
God are generally fulfilled in such
a wondrous manner that He steps
forth to save us at a time when
there is the least appearance of it.

C. H. VON BOGATZKY

Everyday Miracles

Every day holds the possibility of
a miracle. Is it so small a thing to
have enjoyed the sun, to have lived
light in the spring, to have loved,
to have thought, to have done?

MATTHEW ARNOLD

Touch My Heart

Turn my spirit toward You again,
Lord, where I can find the joy and
contentment I'm missing. May I
feel Your Spirit touch my heart,
so that I may bring good to those I
see each day. Amen.

Joy of the Lord

As you wait on the Lord, He
promises to strengthen you
with all might, according to His
glorious power. So what's a little
waiting, as long as God is giving
you strength? And you know
where that strength comes from
after all. . . . The joy of the Lord is
your strength!

JANICE HANNA

Crown of Victory

Battles may be foreseen, and woe to
the man who does not expect them,
but the eye of faith perceives the
crown of victory. Faith is not shelter
against difficulties but belief in the
face of all contradictions.

PAUL TOURNIER

Wings as Eagles

But they that wait upon the LORD
shall renew their strength; they
shall mount up with wings as
eagles; they shall run, and not be
weary; and they shall walk, and not
faint.

ISAIAH 40:31 KJV

Promises Fulfilled

We cannot begin to understand how Your promises are fulfilled, Father, but we know that nothing is impossible for You and all Your promises will come true. All we need is faith.

TONI SORTOR

God's Heart

Grace is no stationary thing; it
is ever becoming. It is flowing
straight out of God's heart. Grace
does nothing but re-form and
convey God. . . . God, the ground
of the soul, and grace go together.

MEISTER ECKHART

Seek Strength

When you feel overburdened,
don't focus on getting out from
under your responsibilities, but ask
the Holy Spirit to build you up in
faith and attentiveness so you can
carry your own load with dignity
and a true appreciation of your
God-given abilities.

REBECCA CURRINGTON AND PATRICIA MITCHELL

Many Wonders

Many, O LORD my God, are the
wonders you have done. The things
you planned for us no one can
recount to you; were I to speak
and tell of them, they would be too
many to declare.

PSALM 40:5 NIV

Our Assurance

Blessed assurance, Jesus is mine!
Oh, what a foretaste
  of glory divine!
Heir of salvation,
  purchase of God,
Born of His Spirit,
  washed in His blood.

FANNY J. CROSBY

Don't Waver

Take each step, obey, and fear not.
One day, one moment at a time is
all He asks. When troubles come,
look to Him, plant your feet on
His path, and dig in. Don't waver!
He'll show the best way. He has
already walked the path.

Christmas Heart

The birth of the baby Jesus stands
as the most significant event in all
history, because it has meant the
pouring into a sick world of the
healing medicine of love which has
transformed all manner of hearts
for almost two thousand years. . . .

GEORGE MATTHEW ADAMS

Keep Christmas

Are you willing to believe that
love is the strongest thing in
the world—stronger than hate,
stronger than evil, stronger than
death—and that the blessed
life which began in Bethlehem
nineteen hundred years ago is
the image and brightness of the
Eternal Love? Then you can keep
Christmas.

HENRY VAN DYKE

Trees Will Clap

"For you will go out with joy
and be led forth with peace; the
mountains and the hills will break
forth into shouts of joy before you,
and all the trees of the field will
clap their hands."

ISAIAH 55:12 NASB

Just like a Child

Heavenly Father, like a child, I do
not always welcome correction.
I pout; I avoid You; I try to go
my own way. In times like those,
please be patient with me. Amen.

Close Enough

We do not need to search for
heaven, over here or over there, in
order to find our eternal Father. In
fact, we do not even need to speak
out loud, for though we speak
in the smallest whisper or the
most fleeting thought, He is close
enough to hear us.

TERESA OF ÁVILA

A Fresh Start

Life in Jesus is all about the
rebirth experience—the
opportunity to start over. Each day
is a new day, in fact. And praise
God! The sorrows and trials of
yesterday are behind us. With each
new morning, joy dawns!

JANICE HANNA

Unconditional and Everlasting Love

Thank You for living water. You are
the Holy One of my life.
As You run an entire universe,
I wonder how You can be
concerned with me. I praise You,
O Lord, that You consider me a
treasure and that You love me with
Your unconditional and everlasting
love.

Scripture Index

Old Testament

NEW TESTAMENT